STUDY-AID SERIES

Notes on Harold Pinter's
THE CARETAKER

Compiled by
A. M. Aylwin, B.A.(London)
Lecturer in English
Avery Hill College of Education, London

Methuen Educational
LONDON · TORONTO · SYDNEY · WELLINGTON

Contents

I	Introduction page	1
II	A look at the text Pinter's use of language	5
III	Structure	8
IV	Style	12
V	Characterization	16
VI	*Any Number of Interpretations* – Some themes in *The Caretaker*	21
VII	Suggestions for essays	27
VIII	Bibliography	28

All rights reserved.
No part of this publication may be reproduced, stored in a retrieval system, or transmitted, in any form or by any means, electronic, mechanical, photocopying, recording or otherwise, without the prior permission of the publisher.

Note: These Notes are published for the use of schools as an aid to the study of English literature for examination purposes. It is important to remember that the Notes serve only as an aid to the study of the book and do not in any way relieve the student of the necessity of reading the original text.

1 Introduction

Harold Pinter was born in Hackney, a working-class area of London, in 1930. He left school at sixteen, and before he was twenty-one he attended intermittently at drama schools in London. In 1951 he began his acting career touring Ireland with a company, and for several years afterwards he acted in repertory theatres in the South of England. He told Laurence Bensky (in an interview in *Paris Review* – see Bibliography) that the boarding house in *The Birthday Party* was based on one where he had stayed in Eastbourne while he was acting in repertory.

His short play *The Room* was produced at Bristol University in 1957. The following year *The Birthday Party* had an unsuccessful run of one week in London.

These early plays came at a time when there was a renewal of interest in the theatre in England. The English Stage Company produced plays by John Osborne, Arnold Wesker, John Arden and many other new young writers at the Royal Court Theatre, and it was a leading influence in encouraging the New Wave of dramatists, as it has been called. Pinter's *The Room* and *The Dumb Waiter* were produced in a double bill at this theatre in 1960.

Many of these new dramatists were strongly critical of society, but Pinter was unusual in this respect. It should be noted, however, that this is no reflection on the strength of Pinter's views about matters of social concern, as the fact that he was a conscientious objector to doing National Service suggests. It is in fact possible to interpret some of his plays as being critical of society, even though the criticism is made obliquely. He told Bensky that he had been influenced at an early age by the writing of Ernest Hemingway and this can be seen in a brief comparison of *The Birthday Party* with Hemingway's short story 'The Killers'. In this story two hired killers arrive in a small American town seeking a man. As the purpose of their visit becomes clear, none of the townspeople attempt to interfere with their plans, and even the victim passively accepts his fate. The story has been interpreted by some as showing the sort of apathy in pre-war society that allowed the Fascists to come to power. The behaviour of Meg and especially of Petey at the end of *The Birthday Party* may imply a similar sort of criticism of people who are afraid of involving themselves in trying to prevent the victimization of other people.

Some of the other writers Pinter mentioned to Bensky as having influenced him have shown a particular interest in the psychology of the human mind. Of these, Pinter said, 'Beckett and Kafka stayed with me most.'

In Kafka's novel *The Trial* a man is accused of an unmentioned crime. He does not know what he is supposed to have done, but nevertheless he feels guilty. In Kafka's short story 'The Metamorphosis' a young man wakes up one morning to find he has been transformed into a giant insect. His horrified family keep him in his room and he finally dies. Both stories may be seen to have something of the feelings of guilt and the nightmare qualities of the *The Birthday Party*.

In Beckett's *Waiting for Godot* two men wait to meet someone called Godot. Although the play is far less naturalistic than *The Caretaker*, we may be reminded of Pinter's play by the fact that the men are tramps and by the references to shoes not fitting. Beckett's theme of salvation and man's hopeless-seeming search for it may be a helpful way of looking at *The Caretaker*.

After the initial failure in London of *The Birthday Party* Pinter became increasingly successful, writing plays for the theatre, radio and television, and also some revue sketches. Since 1962 Pinter has also written the screenplays for several films, has directed plays by other writers and has acted occasionally. He has therefore been connected with so many forms of drama that it is not possible to comment on them all in this small book. Instead reference will be made briefly here to some features of his other works which seem to be relevant to a study of *The Caretaker*. Nevertheless, all Pinter's works demonstrate his interest in the search for the truth that lies beneath outward appearances, the tricks that memory plays and the ways we try to prevent others from knowing what we really think.

The Room (theatre, 1957) – Sarah, a middle-aged housewife, is the central figure in this play. Her fear of the world outside her flat and her unsatisfactory conversation with her husband, Bert, as he reads the paper have much in common with *The Birthday Party*. This play is much more obviously symbolic than Pinter's later plays, and in this respect Bert's obsession with his powerful van suggests perhaps that Goldberg's car and Mick's van are similarly important.

The Birthday Party (theatre, 1958, film 1968)

The Dumb Waiter (theatre, 1959) – In this short play two hired killers wait in an hotel basement to do a job. They are edgy and nervous, feelings which may seem to be a development from the signs of vulnerability of Goldberg and McCann which appear in act three of *The Birthday Party*.

A Slight Ache (radio, 1959; theatre 1961) – The title refers to an ache behind the eyes which a respectable, middle-aged man suffers. As with Stanley Webber, trouble with his eyes is a sign of increasing weakness. It is also another play in which fear of a stranger leads to the central character's collapse.

Revue Sketches (1959) – These include: 'Trouble in the Works', 'The Black and White', 'Request Stop', 'Last to Go' and 'Applicant'.

A Night Out (radio and television, 1960) – This play is about a young man with a mother complex. His inability to break away from his mother may be usefully compared with Stanley's attitude towards Meg and Lulu (*The Birthday Party*).

The Caretaker (theatre 1960: film 1963)

Night School (television 1960)
The Dwarfs (radio 1960) – see the quotation at the end of this section.
The Collection (television 1961; theatre 1962) – In this play a man tries to discover if his wife has been unfaithful to him. It is another play where characters try to unravel fact from fiction without revealing too much of themselves.
The Servant (screenplay for film from Robin Maugham's novel, 1962)
The Lover (television 1963; theatre 1963)
The Pumpkin Eater (screenplay for film from Penelope Mortimer's novel, 1964)
Tea Party (television 1965; theatre 1970)
The Homecoming (theatre 1965) – Teddy, the academic eldest son of a working-class family, brings his wife Ruth back on a visit from America. By the end of the play Teddy has left on his own to rejoin his children while Ruth stays to earn money for the family as a high-class prostitute. The final scene has the father of the family on his knees begging for recognition from Ruth, and the suggestion of the old being replaced by the young is given more emphasis than in *The Caretaker*.
The Quiller Memorandum (screenplay for film from Adam Hall's novel 1966)
The Basement (television 1967; theatre 1970) – A man asks a friend for shelter from the rain and eventually completely takes over his flat.
Accident (screenplay for film from Nicholas Mosley's novel 1967)
Landscape (radio 1968; theatre 1969)
The Go-Between (screenplay for film from L. P. Hartley's novel 1969)
Night (theatre – part of an anthology programme 'Mixed Doubles', 1969)
Silence (theatre 1969)
Old Times (theatre 1971) – It would be interesting to compare Stanley Webber's exit wearing a dark suit (*The Birthday Party*) with the respectability of the forty-year-old Deeley here who looks back on his earlier life unsure whether it was more vital or simply sordid.
No Man's Land (theatre 1975). In this play the shabbily-dressed Spooner is invited back to Hirst's well-furnished house after they have met at a pub. The similarity to *The Caretaker* is striking, but in the later play the characters are, in their intellectual ability, less obviously in need of help. Late in the play, when Spooner asks to be employed as Hirst's secretary, he says: 'If I were wearing a suit such as your own you would see me in a different light.' Could the same be said of Davies (*The Caretaker*)?

Martin Esslin (in W. A. Armstrong's *Experimental Drama*) has drawn a helpful parallel between existentialist philosophy and the works of Samuel Beckett. He writes: 'What is the essence of the experience of being? asks Beckett. And so he begins to strip away the inessentials.' In a less obvious way Pinter may be seen to be doing the same thing, so that the 'inessentials', such as respectable clothes, regular employment and a permanent home, are removed from characters like Stanley Webber and Davies, and we see then their essential characteristics.

The following extracts from a speech by Len in *The Dwarfs* seem to go to the heart of so much of Pinter's writing, and it may be a useful comment to lead into the study of his plays.

'The point is, who are you? Not why or how, not even what. I can see what, perhaps, clearly enough. But who are you? It's no use saying you know who you are just because you tell me you can fit your particular key into a particular slot, which will only receive your particular key because that's not foolproof and certainly not conclusive... What you are, or appear to be to me, or appear to be to you, changes so quickly, so horrifyingly, I certainly can't keep up with it and I'm damn sure you can't either. But who you are I can't even begin to recognize, and sometimes I recognize it so wholly, so forcibly, I can't look, and how can I be certain of what I see? You have no number. Where am I to look, where am I to look, what is there to locate, so as to have some surety, to have some rest from this whole bloody racket? You're the sum of so many reflections. How many reflections? Whose reflections? Is that what you consist of? What scum does the tide leave? What happens to the scum? When does it happen? I've seen what happens. But I can't speak when I see it. I can only point a finger. I can't even do that. The scum is broken and sucked back. I don't see where it goes. I don't see when, what do I see, what have I seen? What have I seen, the scum or the essence? What about it? Does all this give you the right to stand there and tell me you know who you are?'

II A look at the text
Pinter's use of language

In his speech to the National Student Drama Festival at Bristol in 1962, Pinter said: 'There are at least twenty-four possible aspects of any single statement, depending on where you're standing at the time or on what the weather's like. ... No statement I make, therefore, should be interpreted as final and definitive.' (see 'Writing for the Theatre')

Pinter's warning seems appropriate at the start of a study of his work. Although the interpretations of his work by critics sometimes appear to conflict, this should be seen perhaps as reflecting the many-sidedness of the writing. It is to be hoped, too, that nothing in this Study-aid is to be interpreted as 'final and definitive', but that you will make a personal response that arises from a close study of the text and from acting the plays.

This section is intended to indicate certain features of Pinter's use of language in general.

Naturalistic dialogue

Perhaps the first thing one reacts to in a Pinter play is the naturalistic quality of the language. It is no doubt more stylized than real-life conversation for every pause, question and repetition has been carefully placed by Pinter, but we should nevertheless recognize how close we all come to speaking like this at certain times.

The unspoken message What is more difficult to recognize are the thoughts and feelings that underlie the naturalistic dialogue. J. R. Brown has some helpful comments on the work of Stanislavski, one of the most influential drama teachers of this century. He quotes Stanislavski's book *Building a Character* (trans. E. R. Hapgood, Reinhardt & Evans, 1949) thus: 'The spoken word, the text of a play is not valuable in and of itself, but is made so by the inner content of the subtext and what is contained in it . . . Without it the words have no excuse for being presented on the stage.' Pinter, who is also an actor and director of considerable experience, is aware of the importance of the 'subtext', and perhaps the most typical feature of his style is to convey to the audience the contradictory message of a subtext through the naturalistic surface dialogue. Pinter has said: '. . . most of the time we're inexpressive, giving little away, unreliable, elusive, evasive, obstructive, unwilling. But it's out of these attributes that a language arises. A language, I repeat, where, under what is said, another thing is being said . . .' ('Writing for the Theatre')

It might help towards understanding Pinter's techniques if students improvised conversations similar to those used by Pinter. For example, one might create a family breakfast scene or a scene where two or three people meet at a party. If it is possible to tape-record this, then a follow-up activity can be to repeat the conversation keeping almost the same words but with one of the characters under great tension, for example, a wife who has decided to leave her husband.

Pinter brings out these inner tensions by a variety of techniques.

Questions Pinter's plays are filled with questions which imply much more than simply the seeking of information. Most frequently the questioner is asserting his authority. Mick's questioning of Davies in *The Caretaker* suggests this. Sometimes the questions reveal insecurity and nervousness. Davies's questioning of Aston in *The Caretaker* may be a mixture of insecure feelings and a desire to take control.

Repetition This may sometimes reveal a paucity of vocabulary, Davies being the obvious example.

Silences and pauses In his 1962 speech at Bristol Pinter said: 'I think that we communicate only too well, in our silence, in what is unsaid, and that what takes place is continual evasion, desperate rearguard attempts to keep ourselves. Communication is too alarming. To enter into someone else's life is too frightening. To disclose to others the poverty within us is too fearsome a possibility.' Close attention should be paid to the words which follow the stage direction 'Pause'. Pinter has said: 'The pause is a pause, because of what has just happened in the minds and guts of the characters.' (Interview with Mel Gussow, *New York Times Magazine*, Dec. 1971) The reasons for such pauses are therefore many and varied.

Actions Words and silences are sometimes accompanied by actions which give added significance. Davies's punching downward with his fist tells us a lot about his feelings, (p.10). The positioning of characters can also be significant as in the closing moments of *The Caretaker* as Aston remains at the window with his back to Davies.

Unusual language

Dialogue in Pinter's early plays tends to be between characters who can manipulate language to serve their own ends and characters who cannot match them with words.

Inarticulate language Pinter has said: 'The more intense the feeling, the less articulate its expression.'

A torrent of language In his 1962 Bristol speech Pinter said: 'There are two silences. One when no word is spoken. The other when perhaps a torrent of language is being employed. This speech is speaking of a language locked beneath it. That is its continual reference. The speech we hear is an indication of what we don't hear.' In *The Caretaker* Mick asserts his authority over Davies with a long rapid speech about his 'uncle's brother' (p.31). Torrents of language can also be used to disguise anxiety.

Articulate language Command of language often implies authority. In *The Caretaker*, as Davies struggles to find a word to describe Mick, the latter provides the word, 'Straightforward'. (p.61)

Consistency of language to character Perhaps the most remarkable feature of Pinter's dialogue is that in spite of the great variety of its language styles, characters do retain a consistency of style which adds to the realistic qualities of the plays.

When one recognizes the essential qualities of a character and through them the consistency of his behaviour in terms of character, then it becomes possible to explain all his language, although with the twenty-four possible aspects it is unlikely that we will always agree.

However, on this question of interpreting the language of his plays, Pinter has given some wise advice in a speech in Hamburg, 1970: 'Sometimes, the director says to me in rehearsal: "Why does she say this?" I reply: "Wait a minute, let me look at the text." I do so, and perhaps I say: "Doesn't she say this because he said *that*, two pages ago?" Or I say: "Because that's what she feels." Or: "Because she feels something else, and therefore says that." Or: "I haven't the faintest idea. But somehow we have to find out." '

III Structure

> ... that's my main concern, to get the structure right
> (Interview with L. Bensky, Oct. 1966)

As indicated in section two, Pinter's use of language is of prime importance in a study of his plays, and it influences all aspects under discussion in this book. The division into sections is, therefore, somewhat arbitrary.

In a B.B.C. radio interview with Kenneth Tynan (28th October 1960), Pinter said: 'I start writing a play from an image of a situation and a couple of characters involved, and these people remain for me quite real; if they were not, the play could not be written.'

The structure of *The Caretaker* seems to be shaped to a large extent by the behaviour of the characters which makes for less obvious patterning than we find, for example, in *The Birthday Party* with its opening and closing scenes. In this sense it is a naturalistic play, although the characters are unusual. It is perhaps significant that Davies says, 'I don't dream. I've never dreamed', and Aston replies, 'No, nor have I.' (22)

The naturalistic and the extraordinary

The story of *The Caretaker* is quite clear. An old tramp-like man, Davies, has lost his job in a café and been saved from a beating by a man, Aston, who invites him back to his room. Aston has been unable to work for years since receiving electric treatment for a mental illness. He plans to build a work-shed and make alterations on the house. Meanwhile, his younger brother, Mick, keeps an eye on him. When Aston invites Davies to stay, Mick alarms the old man and then traps him into turning against Aston so that both brothers realize that they do not want him in the house.

The audience's first impression of the play, however, is that it is far from naturalistic. The room is more like a store-room full of old furniture than a bedroom, and the mysterious presence and departure of Mick are unexplained when Aston and Davies enter.

Davies is immediately recognizable as a lazy, disgruntled man who lives by casual work. He seems a figure to despise as we learn about him from his own outpouring of complaints. Even his attempts at disguising the truth are transparently false, as when he says: 'I've had dinner with the best.' (9)

Aston's plain style of speech may prevent him appearing as a mysterious figure, and Davies asks few questions about him, but why he should be living in this condition is not clear until the end of act two (54–57). The mystery of Mick, in fact, is cleared up before this. Mick's attack on Davies at the end of act one (28) and the stream of questions and nonsensical phrases he flings at Davies demonstrate his familiarity with the place and a sense of his power without telling us who he is. We learn this when Aston says, 'He's my brother.' (39) From this point on there is no mystery of the sort that there is in *The Birthday Party* concerning the visitors. Mick, indeed, now goes on to tell Davies that he is the landlord (51), and so with the removal of the mystery surrounding him, he perhaps increases his authority.

Aston's extraordinary background is revealed in his speech about the terrible treatment he has received in a mental hospital (54—57). It is this revelation that decides Davies to commit himself to obeying Mick.

There are no more revelations in act three. We have come to know all three characters, and in the fluctuating moods of this act all are consistently in character. That the structure of the play has been determined by the development of the characters is made clear by Pinter in an interview (*New Theatre Magazine*, 1961) when he said:

> I thought originally that the play must end with the violent death of one at the hands of the other. But then I realized, when I got to the point, that the characters as they had grown could never act in this way.

In the final moments of the play, then, the extraordinary features of character and setting are subordinate to the naturalistic demonstration of human behaviour.

Patterns

Because the behaviour of the characters has an inner consistency, the play as a whole has a structure which contains fluctuating movements largely caused by the deliberate efforts of Davies and Mick to manoeuvre Aston and each other to suit their purposes.

The slow build-up of act one with Davies's rambling talk and Aston's brief remarks is surrounded by the silent opening scene with Mick alone on stage and the closing scene with Mick attacking Davies. The opening scene may condition our response as to how we hear Aston and Davies.

During his conversation with Aston, Davies reveals his fear of the outside world, expressed by his references to foreigners (8, 13, 14, 18 and 27). The occasional glances out of the window (17, 24 and 54) are reminders of this outside world with the Indian neighbours and the work needed to be done in the garden. These moments glancing through the window also prepare us for the final scene as Aston looks out at the garden and Davies has to face going out once more into that hostile world.

Davies's anxious question, 'You don't share it, do you?' (18) comes mid-way through this act and may remind us of Mick's presence earlier. His anxiety here is about 'them Blacks' and is unfounded. As his confidence increases and he begins to explore the room, the mood of relative calm is shattered by Mick's attack.

The end of act one prepares us for the bewilderment and fear that Davies shows in the opening moments of act two. Likewise, Aston's long speech at the end of act two helps to explain the new-found confidence of Davies at the start of act three.

Once Mick has entered fully into the action we see that his behaviour is in great contrast to Aston's, and the way the two brothers touch on similar subjects when they talk to Davies helps to give a unity to the structure of the play. For example, Mick's question, 'Who do you bank with?' (36) may be compared with Aston's gift of five shillings (19). Davies's fear of the apparently more powerful brother causes him to choose the wrong master. When Aston offers him a job (42), he is unsure. Soon after this Mick first frightens Davies in the dark with the vacuum cleaner (45) and then indicates that Davies is only there temporarily by asking, 'How long you thinking of staying here by the way?' (46). Having reminded Davies of his insecure position, Mick, surprisingly, soon goes on to offer him the job of caretaker as well (50), and this time Davies 'decisively' accepts it (51). Davies is to realize his mistake too late, and in the final moments of the play he makes an offer to Aston to 'look after the place for you . . . not for . . . for your brother' (76).

The play is also given unity by the interaction between each brother and Davies, for the old man moves from one to the other from the end of act one onwards. The importance of Aston's speech at the end of act two is emphasized because it breaks the normal rhythms of his conversations with Davies and because the fading light leaves him isolated (54). Aston and Mick are only seen together twice, but significantly Davies is shown to be outside their relationship. On the first occasion the brothers talk about the leaking roof, apparently ignoring Davies (37). Later, after Mick has told Davies that he does not want to employ him, he exchanges a faint smile with Aston on leaving the room. Thus, although Davies has been moving from one brother to the other as if moving between extremes, we are finally left perhaps with a sense of the brothers' closeness to each other.

The influence of the language on the structure

The Caretaker builds up in intensity throughout the play, and this effect is largely achieved by its language. One has only to examine Davies's vicious speech against Aston (66, 67) to see how much he has changed. It has already been shown above how the recurrence of words, as in the offer of the caretaking job, contribute to the play's unity. The gathering intensity of the play is also influenced by the repetition of words, as the following examples illustrate.

When Davies first mentions Aston's bed he says, 'Yes, well, you'd be well out of the draught there.' (11) He goes on to say how sleeping out 'Gets very draughty.' He seems to be hinting at being offered a bed here. When he does get into bed his first remark is, 'Not bad. Not bad. A fair bed. I think I'll sleep in this' (21), and next morning when Aston suggests the bed may have made him dream, he replies, 'Nothing wrong with this bed.' (23) When Mick arrives to bewilder him with a nonsensical deluge of words, Davies answers three times that he has slept well (30, 32, 33). Up to this point, then, Davies has no complaints to make about the bed.

Mick's remark, 'You want to mind you don't catch a draught' (33), momentarily brings Davies back to his earlier comment on bad places for sleeping, (11) but Mick is only preparing the way for an unpleasant joke which is to be understood as a threat. Next morning, as a counter to Aston's complaint about his noises during the night, Davies says, 'Draught's blowing right in on my head, anyway.' (52) This leads to a dispute about whether the window should be closed or not. Mick's description of the place as a 'penthouse' (60) illustrates most clearly the importance of the beds. He says, 'What's a bedroom? It's a retreat. It's a place to go for rest and peace.' This describes what Davies found at the start of act one, and what Aston is now failing to have. Aston's preference for an open window may be indirectly related to his efforts to saw through the bars of the hospital window (56), but it is clearly explained when, after he has been provoked by Davies's reference to his 'stinking shed' (68), he tells the old man, 'You've been stinking the place out.' (69) Davies is insulted and complains to Mick who appears to sympathize, saying, 'If you stank I'd be the first one to tell you.' (70) However, Mick has already told Davies, 'You're stinking the place out' (35), and we can see that he is once more trapping Davies into a complete betrayal of Aston's friendship. When he makes his final verbal onslaught on Davies, Mick uses the word 'stink' even more unpleasantly (74).

That Davies has still not understood how he has offended Aston is shown in the closing moments of the play when he says, 'You didn't mean that, did you, about me stinking, did you?' (75), and he again blames the draught for causing him to sleep badly. His final suggestion is to put a stronger piece of sacking over the window, again with the purpose of preventing the draught (77).

Such uses of language intensify the dramatic tension as the action proceeds. There are other examples of a similar nature. Note, for instance, the use of 'animal' (15, 67 and 73). The final effect is to show us how unworthy Davies is of any friendship, before he makes his appeal for that very thing.

IV Style

Language

The following comments are closely linked with those in section two of these notes.

The difference between the brothers is strikingly shown in the way they talk. Mick's language often includes elaborate words and phrases, as, for example, when he describes how he could alter the house (60), whereas Aston's remarks are usually brief and simply phrased. In his inarticulate, hesitant speech Davies is closer to Aston, but his search for more impressive-sounding words, such as 'aliens' (8) and 'implements' (43) indicate why he is so impressed by Mick.

Davies's sort of inarticulate language is appropriate to the tramp-like figure he is. When Aston gives him money, he replies, 'Thank you, thank you, good luck.' (19) His way of addressing people also seems appropriate to one who often begs favours from strangers. When he receives gifts from Aston (8, 16 and 19), he uses the word 'mister' in replying, and does the same when Mick gives him a sandwich (47). At such moments he reveals his feelings of inferiority, and his attitude towards society is shown in his speech about answering the door-bell, in which the word 'they' is used five times (44). He seems to spend his life avoiding working responsibly and cadging food and clothes, and his evasive manner of speaking reflects this. Note his way of avoiding Aston's question, 'Where were you born then?' (25), and Aston's question about the 'caff' in Wembley (27).

This evasiveness is so deeply ingrained in his manner, it seems, that he frequently responds to a question with another question, as if he needs time to understand the implications behind the words. When Aston asks if he wants a cigarette, he immediately says, 'What?' (8), and this is typical of him. He can cope neither with simple language whether used by Aston or Mick nor with elaborate language, and instead uses a repetitive style in his unsuccessful efforts to find the right words. The people in the cafe he describes angrily as, 'All them Greeks had it, Poles, Greeks, Blacks, the lot of them, all of them aliens had it' (8), and he follows this with a similar list, repeating 'Blacks' twice. Of his worn-out shoes he says, 'they're gone, they're no good, all the good's gone out of them' (15), rewording the phrase perhaps in an effort to impress Aston.

Mick's use of language is in striking contrast to both Davies's and Aston's, especially at the start of act two when we first hear him in full flow. Pinter told Bensky, 'Too many words irritate me sometimes, but I can't help them, they just seem to come out — out of the fellow's mouth. I don't really examine my words too much, but I am aware that quite often in what I write some fellow at some point says an awful lot.' Mick's speeches are indeed often long and nonsensical, but we may sense that he is deliberately trying to confuse Davies, so that unusual, high-sounding words like 'penchant' (31) help him to achieve his intended aim. There is a feeling of natural inventiveness about his speech, because it seems as if one idea leads him on to another. See, for example, his description of the bus routes (32). Although Mick's early speeches stress his recognition of the sort of man Davies is, when he goes on to talk about the house (35, 36) his long speech is filled with financial and legal terms. By these means he emphasizes how far Davies is from having any right to stay there. Even more significant perhaps are the expressions referring to crime and punishment that are slipped in, such as: 'loitering with intent', 'remission of term for good behaviour' and 'carry the can' (all on 36).

Such terms from the world of crime link with the style of the cross-examination which Mick adopts when questioning Davies, as when he repeats, 'What's your name?' (30 and 32). Such implied violence also underlies some of the language. 'Sorted out' and 'fixed up' (16, 21 and 63), used in referring to Davies's employment, may both carry a suggestion of violence, and that Davies understands the violent meanings becomes clear in his use of them to Aston when he says, 'They'd keep you fixed!' (67) and 'he'll sort you out' (69). There is also an implied threat perhaps in Mick's expression 'a good going over' (45).

Aston's style of speech also reveals much about him and the effect the hospital treatment has had on him. He is not inarticulate like Davies, however, and his careful searching for the right words possibly gives a feeling that he is slowly moving towards recovery and self-sufficiency.

Between the words

The following comments are also closely linked with those in section two.

John Russell Taylor has quoted Pinter as saying, 'Life is much more mysterious than plays make it out to be. And it is this mystery which fascinates me; what happens between the words, what happens when no words are spoken.' (In 'Accident', *Sight and Sound*, Autumn, 1966).

It should be noted that in *The Caretaker* there are frequent pauses within the speeches of both Aston and Davies. Davies often hesitates in an effort to avoid revealing too much of himself, as when Aston asks him if he is Welsh. There is pause before Davies replies, 'Well, I been around, you know . . . what I mean . . . I been about . . .' (25). At other times, Davies's hesitations, rather than being the results of his avoiding an answer, are signs of his indirect way of asking for something. An example of this comes where he seems to be hinting that he would like to stay. After his words about sleeping out-of-doors, 'Nothing but wind then' (11), there are nine pauses indicated in little more than a page of the text. Other pauses come where Davies is too shocked to speak, as when Mick says that he and his brother would be the ones to live in the altered flat (61). After a pause, Davies says, 'What about me?', a question he repeats when Mick finally leaves (74). There is a similar sense of shock for Aston in the silence which follows his words, 'That's not a stinking shed.' (68)

Periods of silence occur throughout the play which is indeed framed, as it were, by two silences, the first when Mick's presence gives a sense of his power, the last when Aston stands with his back to Davies refusing to answer his plea to be taken back. The fact that act two begins 'A few seconds' after the end of act one makes the break between the acts a sort of extended silence after Mick's question, 'What's the game?' The length of this silence in the theatre should increase the audience's awareness of Davies's sense of panic.

Atmosphere

Although there is an atmosphere of menace in *The Caretaker* as in Pinter's earlier plays, everything unusual can here be given a satisfactory explanation in naturalistic terms. Of this play, Pinter told Kenneth Tynan (B.B.C., Oct. 1960), 'I have no need to use cabaret turns and blackouts and screams in the dark to the extent that I enjoyed using them before. I feel I can deal, without resorting to that kind of thing, with a human situation.' Whereas in *The Birthday Party* the blackout is rather unsatisfactorily explained by the meter needing a shilling in the slot, in *The Caretaker* we sense that Mick has deliberately removed the light bulb in order to frighten Davies (45).

However, lighting effects are used more symbolically when Aston makes his long speech (54–57), the light slowly fading to leave the spotlight on him in his isolation. The chaotic state of the room may also be seen as a symbol of Aston's life, and, in the stove especially, it also carries a sense of menace for Davies.

Clothes

Pinter's stage directions about clothing are more detailed here than they are in most of his earlier plays. Mick's leather jacket and Aston's suit seem most appropriate. Most significant is the change we see in Davies. His shabby appearance at the start is transformed by act three where we see him 'sitting in the chair, holding his pipe . . . wearing the smoking jacket' (58).

Ironically, Aston's kindness has equipped him with better shoes for the new travels which it seems he will have to undertake. It is ironic, too, that Mick should threaten him by snatching his trousers, thereby preventing him from leaving.

Actions

The bag which Aston brings back for Davies contains clothes, and it immediately brings the three characters together in a struggle where Davies's only concern is to receive the bag for himself, while Mick interferes with Aston's offer. How should we interpret the fact that it is Mick who finally gives the bag to Davies?

Other objects emphasize the relative strengths of Davies and Mick. Davies threatens both Mick and Aston with his knife (45/46 and 67–69), and neither is alarmed, whereas Mick frightens Davies with his foot (29), his trousers (34) and the electrolux (45). Aston's own concern to rehabilitate himself is perhaps suggested by his attempts to repair the toaster, and that he seems to have repaired the roof later (58) may be seen as a hopeful sign. Davies, however, apart from brandishing the knife and trying on clothes and shoes, has little to occupy his hands.

Davies's most expressive use of his hands indeed comes in gestures which, replacing the words he cannot find, show his frustration and fear as he 'punches downward with closed fist' (8) and as he starts 'banging on the floor' (33). In the latter case he is lying on the floor dominated by Mick, and it is also worth noting the positions of the characters in relation to each other as they sit, stand or lie down at different times in the play.

'What's funny about that?' (Mick, p.50)

Studying a set text for an exam is enough perhaps to deaden the effect of any comedy, but the importance of the rich humour of *The Caretaker* should always be kept in mind. Pinter has said, 'The point about tragedy is that it is *no longer funny*. It is funny, and then it becomes no longer funny.' (quoted by Esslin in *The Theatre of the Absurd*, p.212).

On first experiencing *The Caretaker* one is likely to find much of act one very funny. The very sight of Davies makes his assertion, 'I'm clean' (9), a comic contradiction. His description of his visit to a monastery has the comic shock of the crude expression, 'Piss off' (14), allegedly spoken by a monk. His concern about the stove and the Blacks, and his account of his change of name and need for his papers in Sidcup all help to create a comic feeling which, however, is not recognized by the two characters involved. They are almost like music-hall comedians who keep straight faces while the audience laugh.

However, Pinter has written (in a letter to *The Times*, August 14, 1960), 'As far as I'm concerned *The Caretaker* is funny up to a point. Beyond that point it ceases to be funny, and it was because of that point that I wrote it.'

The type of humour that Mick brings in act two is very different from the earlier humour. He clearly takes a delight in his comic outpouring of words, though Davies is merely bewildered. His speech about his 'uncle's brother' (31) refers to him being 'chucked ... out of the Salvation Army', and in his next speech the words, 'That didn't make any difference to me' (32), seem quite inappropriate to the relatively smart district of Putney. Mick's frightening Davies with the electrolux is also comic, but we soon see that there is a terrifying quality to his style of humour which has something of the delight of the tormentor in it. Pinter told Bensky that a funny speech often conceals the desperate condition of the speaker ('... more often than not the speech only *seems* to be funny – the man in question is actually fighting a battle for his life.'). With this comment in mind you should perhaps consider whether Mick himself is also 'fighting a battle for his life'.

V Characterization

I like to create character and follow situation to its end.
(Interview in *The New Yorker*, February 25, 1967)

General remarks

Pinter's characters may seem, on the whole, extraordinary and, in this respect, contradictions of his expressed interest in them as living people. The explanation for this would seem to lie in what he told Kenneth Tynan, 'I'm dealing with these characters at the extreme edge of their living, where they are living pretty much alone, at their heart, their home hearth.' (B.B.C., October 28, 1960).

As his characters are placed under great pressure, it becomes harder to predict how they will react, so it is not surprising to find Pinter saying, 'Characters always grow out of all proportion to your original conception of them, and if they don't the play is a bad one.' (*New Theatre Magazine*, 1961)

It is Pinter's interest in his characters as living people that helps him follow their likely reactions rather than any preconceived plan. In his 1962 Bristol speech, he said of his method of characterization, 'Given characters who possess a momentum of their own, my job is not to impose upon them, not to subject them to false articulation, by which I mean forcing a character to speak where he could not speak, of making him speak of what he could never speak.'

At certain times some characters know no more about what is happening than does the audience.

To understand the signifance of the speech of Pinter's characters, then, we have to be sensitive to the 'language locked beneath it'.

Paradoxically, it is perhaps the very elusiveness of Pinter's characters which gives them the life-like qualities with which we may find we can sympathize.

The following notes will concentrate on the portrayal of the characters as life-like people. Other interpretations of their parts in the play will follow in section six.

Although the title of *The Caretaker* emphasizes the role of Davies, our sympathy may be given to all three characters. Pinter has said that his characters seem to grow as if they were living people during the composition of a play, and this seems to be particularly true of *The Caretaker*. What do you think your attitude would be towards the three characters if Davies were forced to leave for ever by Mick at the start of act two?

Davies

By the end of the play Davies seems a most unlikely character to win our sympathy. That he may do so is the result of our understanding both of his predicament and of his consequent behaviour.

As a sort of tramp who seeks a home, he may gain our sympathy at once, of course, and his interest in shoes and soap (13) helps to show him to be like this. When he has found a room to stay in, his locking the door and searching through the contents (28) may make him seem to be dishonest, but after his hesitation over sitting down (8) and over accepting a bed for the night (16), he may be seen to be a man who has become suspicious of any kindness shown towards him.

His experience of life has made him expect the worst, as we see when he wakes up, momentarily forgetting where he is (22). He is alarmed about the neighbours (12), and inside the room he is afraid of the fire and the gas stove (26). His fear of such things suggests that he cannot cope with modern living, and Mick plays on this fear when he uses the electrolux (45). That he is unsure of what to do is frequently shown in his hesitant questions, such as when he asks where to put his trousers (21), and his inarticulate speech reveals this throughout the play.

His feelings of insecurity explain his questions about who is in charge (12 and 51), and when he thinks he knows' he behaves in a humble, even servile, manner. Nevertheless, he does see himself as being worth something and this accounts for his complaints about being unfairly treated, especially by people who are not sufficiently superior. He says the Scot who ordered him to carry the bucket was 'not my boss' (10), and the menial nature of the task shows how desperately near he feels to being at the bottom of the social scale. It is this feeling that causes him to despise others, such as Blacks and Greeks (8). His greediness, for example, in demanding the bag Aston brings back (38), or in asking Aston for money (26), also arises partly from the sort of life he leads.

His poverty-stricken life may also excuse, to some extent, his habit of complaining, even when his reasons seem nonsensical, as when he criticizes check shirts (41). His preference here for 'a shirt with stripes', however, also has in its illogicality something recognizably human about it, and his moments of self-pity are common to many people. He says he is old (10, 14 and 66), has been ill (9) and was underpaid (19).

Because Davies lays claim to having some dignity, he is humiliated by the work he is forced to do in the café (8). In self-defence he either lies or deceives himself about his life. He claims to have had 'dinner with the best' (9), and apparently fails to see the irony in Mick's criticism of Aston as someone who does not like work (48). It is this sort of self-deception that leads to him complaining that Aston is 'Treating (him) like dirt!' (67)

The open criticism that Davies makes against Aston in act three has a vicious quality that has been apparent at times earlier in the play. He says that he will revenge himself one night on the 'Scotchman' in the cafe (10), and twice he brandishes a knife (45 and 67). Less forgivable, however, is the way he takes advantage of Aston's generosity and his attempt to displace him.

We last see him making his pathetic attempt to be taken back by Aston.

He ends once more as the outsider we have seen him to be before when the brothers have ignored him (37).

Aston

Of the three characters, we are most likely to feel sympathy for Aston whose generosity is soon apparent when he offers Davies a cigarette (8), a pair of shoes (14), a bed (16) and money (19). It is perhaps Davies's acceptance of these offers that leads Aston to reveal some of his feelings and experiences of life in remarks about the Buddha (17), the Guinness (19), the woman in the café (24/25), his hopes for the shed (40) and finally his experience in the hospital (54–57).

His treatment in the hospital appears to have dulled his former sensitivity, and he needs to talk about it to come to terms with his present life. His working on the electric plug may be linked with his trying to understand the electric treatment he has had. The white coat that he offers Davies when asking him if he would like to be caretaker may throw a different light on how he sees Davies, for a doctor wears a white coat and takes care of people. Davies's refusal to work for him may therefore be seen as giving Aston a new sense of freedom.

He blames his mother for signing a hospital form giving permission for his operation (56), and the possibility that he sleeps in her bed (35) suggests that he may still be under her influence, even though there is no mention in the play of her still being alive. The doctor has said, 'You can go out ... and live like the others' (55), and his 'dark-blue pinstripe suit' (7) suggests this sort of conformity (although it may also remind us of Stanley at the end of *The Birthday Party*). Nevertheless, he seems to have withdrawn from society, and he says, 'I don't talk to people now.' (57) It seems that the doctor was wrong, for there are still signs in Aston of the extreme sensitivity that the operation was presumably intended to deaden, as suggested by his purchase of the Buddha and his dislike of drinking from a thick mug (19). His sensitivity may make it harder for him to tolerate Davies's noises at night. However, he has felt sympathy for Davies, perhaps as a result of his own painful experiences in a café (54/55), and he tries to come to the old man's rescue when Mick torments him with the bag by saying, 'Scrub it.' (38)

His plain speaking here to Mick is typical of him in the rest of the play. When Davies asks about the bucket, Aston simply replies, 'Leak.' (21) His comments about Davies making noises in his sleep also show his plain speaking, but Davies finds them difficult to accept (22/23). However, he does not easily take offence, and Davies's abuse of his generosity by asking for money receives the simple, though strong, reply, 'I gave you a few bob yesterday.' (26) His speech is as matter-of-fact when he is with Mick, and we may feel it is ironic that Davies should call Mick 'straightforward' (61).

However, in the interview with Bensky, Pinter sounds a note of caution on the interpretation of Aston's speech about the mental hospital, saying,

'I had no axe to grind there. And the one thing that people have missed is that it isn't necessary to conclude that everything Aston says about his experiences in the mental hospital is true.' Is it possible, then, that Aston sets out to revenge himself on society by hurting Davies?

What does seem to happen to Aston during the course of the play is a gradual growth of confidence in his ability to manage on his own. When Davies switches allegiance to Mick we find that Aston appears to have mended the roof (58), and when Davies makes his final appeal to be taken back, Aston turns away towards the window saying, 'I've got that shed to get up.' (76) Before his long speech we have seen him mending a plug or sandpapering wood (52). His final looking out into the garden is perhaps a sign that he will make a start at last.

Nevertheless, some have seen the end of the play as tragic for Aston in particular, for he has been forced to act against his own natural generosity in rejecting Davies.

Mick

Of the three men, Mick is the only one to have a job, and although we don't know exactly what it is, he does have his own van, it seems (40). The film version of the play, with Pinter's approval, made this clear by showing Mick driving his van. The fluency of some of his speeches suggests that he has experience of buildings and property. It may also be felt that his experience in his work make him especially frustrated at seeing the chaotic state of the room Aston is living in. Although his words are presumably mainly designed to confuse Davies, they may also show him as a dreamer in his ideas about how the flat could be converted (60).

That he has the ability to realize such a dream is suggested by his obvious power, for example, in his attack on Davies at the end of act one (28), and this is combined with a malevolent sense of humour that has Davies completely at his mercy when he cross-questions him at the start of act two (30–36).

Nevertheless, despite the pleasure he seems to take in baiting Davies, there is often a sense of dissatisfaction in his words, which may be felt when Aston tells him how he will patch up the roof (37). This dissatisfaction reaches a climax when he smashes the Buddha and denies any more responsibility for Aston (74). His own dreams of a 'penthouse' (60) are far removed from Aston's ideas, and he may even be seen to represent the sort of society that Aston has deliberately withdrawn from. He may also be frustrated by his duty to look after Aston, for he is the younger brother.

However, we need to look closely at the scenes where Mick and Aston are present. For example, Mick lets Davies have his trousers back as soon as Aston enters (36), and he finally allows Davies to have the bag, though it should be noted that he is the one to give it (39). It is conceivable that he is jealous of the attention Davies is receiving from Aston. He could have driven Davies away earlier (34) but chooses to lure the old man into turning against Aston, thereby forcing Aston to be the one who finally rejects him.

He complains about Aston to Davies for doing no work (48), and when Davies begins to criticize Aston, Mick does not object (58/59). His distrust of Davies, shown at once in his question, 'What's the game' (29), is perhaps a sign of his fear of being replaced himself.

Just what Mick's relationship with Aston is, is hard to decide. When Mick demands to know Davies's two names (73), it seems as if Aston has informed him about the old man's earlier explanation. This would suggest that the brothers have met elsewhere during the action of the play. Moreover, the faint smile they exchange before Mick finally leaves (75) suggests that they share an understanding from which Davies is excluded. There is even a possibility, though a very faint one, that the tormenting of Davies has been planned by both of them. More likely is the conclusion that Aston acknowledges at last the treachery in Davies that Mick may have been warning him against. Mick, though still burdened with the responsibility of caring for his brother, can once more feel that Aston is safe from the abuses of greedy strangers.

VI Some themes in *The Caretaker* —
Any Number of Interpretations

General remarks

Mick tells Davies in act three, 'Every word you speak is open to any number of interpretations' (73), and his words here seem an appropriate comment on the language of the whole play. Consequently, it is not surprising to find critics interpreting the play in different ways. As already suggested, developing a receptive ear for Pinter's language is essential to appreciating his plays. To avoid repetition little more will be said on this aspect of his work. Three themes will be examined in some detail in this section, after a brief look at some of the many other ways in which the play may be interpreted.

Most closely connected with the use of language is the theme of *communication*. Undoubtedly, in their different ways, Aston and Davies are trying to communicate with each other at the start of the play. Davies, however, perhaps communicates unintentionally what he wants to hide. Pinter has expressed his dislike of the 'grimy, tired phrase, failure of communication', indicating that it is in our attempts to avoid being known that we 'communicate only too well' ('Writing for the Theatre'). In a different way, Mick uses a torrent of elaborate language about interior decorating to communicate his hostility to Davies.

In Mick's case, the use of language helps to express his plans for the future. His exaggeration (60) makes the realization of these plans most unlikely, and this may be seen as part of a theme of *illusion*, which includes Davies's excuse that his papers are in Sidcup, and Aston's belief that once he has built his shed he will get started.

There have been some interpretations of the play in terms of allegory. Clifford Leech, for example, sees Davies as an Everyman figure wandering through the world, with the two brothers as bright and dark angels. Pinter has resisted such ideas, and in reply to Terence Rattigan's interpretation of the play in similar terms, he reputedly said, 'It's about two brothers and a caretaker.'

In a very different way, *The Caretaker* can be studied for its implied *social criticism*, although, as the interest is always so much on the individual, it is perhaps unwise to stress this too much. In this respect one might consider what society has done to Aston in the hospital, and Davies's racial intolerance and his later cruelty towards Aston.

Davies's intolerance is linked also with the theme of *menace* which, if less apparent than in Pinter's earlier plays, is still part of this play. Davies is afraid of things that he does not understand, such as the unconnected gas stove; Aston is haunted by memories of his past in hospital. Mick is more obviously seen as actively menacing Davies, but his behaviour may suggest his own fear that he is going to lose his place in his brother's affections.

The following three themes, which are discussed in more detail, illustrate the difficulty of trying to separate different aspects of Pinter's work. In turn, they represent an attempt to see the play first from the point of view of the brothers, then from Davies's point of view, before a look at the relationship of Aston and Davies brings the first two interpretations together.

'Of course, there's a lot to be done to this place' (Aston, p.41)

Although many of Pinter's early plays are set in one room only, the room in *The Caretaker* is rather different from the others. We see at once that it is in a chaotic state. An extraordinary variety of objects clutters up the room, most of them obviously not in use. It is in this room that Aston sleeps. When Davies comments on the amount of furniture there, Aston says, 'Just keeping it here for the time being.' (16) This suggests that at this point Aston is unsure about where to start on his alterations, even though he mentions his intention of building a shed in the overgrown garden with quiet determination, saying, 'I'll get it done.' (17)

The arrival of Davies could perhaps be seen as an additional useless object to the room, or as an attempt by Aston to enlist support from a fellow human being. Davies's acceptance of shelter leads to a re-ordering of the room to uncover the second bed (18), but the room remains as chaotic in appearance. Aston's efforts to improve the room seem rather ineffectual. He examines and pokes the electric plug at different times in the play (19, 21, 22, 42 and 75), yet we do not see it repaired. The bucket hangs from the ceiling to catch drips from the leaking roof (21). He can make neither tea (17) nor toast (22) in the room. Mick later questions Aston about how he intends to repair the roof (37), and again Aston uses the phrase 'for the time being' suggesting that something better will be done when he is ready to start work properly.

Aston states his plans more clearly after Mick has left (40/41), referring to the shed and to putting a partition in one of the rooms. Does the partition suggest a wish to separate himself, and if so, from what or whom?

In spite of Aston's plans, we become increasingly aware of Mick's claims on the house after he has said, 'How do you like my room?' (31) He tells Davies that he is 'responsible for the upkeep of the premises' (46). Mick's responsibility seems more likely after Aston's speech about his hospital treatment (54–57). Aston's life has fallen into ruins and he feels he can accomplish nothing now until he has built his shed in the garden. Mick, therefore, may have the responsibility of helping Aston to look after the house until he can manage on his own.

The building of the shed and the alterations to the house may thus be seen as symbolic of Aston's need to get his chaotic state of mind into order, so that he can cope once more with life. There are signs that he is making a start, for he appears to have stopped the leak (58). In act three, Mick also shows a desire to alter the house. His ideas are wildly extravagant, and the jargon of interior decorating that he uses shows how different he is from Aston. Yet Aston, in his appreciation of the Buddha (17), has perhaps shown a deeper sense of artistic taste than Mick. Martin Esslin gives one interpretation of Aston as, 'an artistic personality forcibly reduced to sober respectability', and compares him with the musically-gifted Stanley in *The Birthday Party*. Yet how does one interpret the smashing of the Buddha? (74) Does the sight of the broken pieces give Aston the freedom to start his practical job on the shed? Does it free him from any sense of attachment to Davies, or reliance on his brother? It should be noted that Mick leaves before Aston sees the broken Buddha (75).

Finally, Davies, who is earlier brought into the room like an addition to its useless furniture, is turned out as being no longer wanted. His rejection is perhaps an indication that Aston can now accept full responsibility for his life, and so is ready to make a start on his shed.

'You don't belong in a nice place like this' (Mick, p.35)

The place that Mick refers to is far from 'nice', as we can see, but Davies's desperate wish to 'belong' somewhere seems to be an important idea in the play. It is clear that his life has consisted of moving from one unsatisfactory place to another. Aston's invitation to him to come back to the house seems to have given him the rare chance of having a home. That the home is an unusual one is felt by Davies as well as by the audience, and we see this when he questions Aston about the house, neighbours (11, 12), garden (17) and stove (26). When he is left on his own in the room he examines its contents, and says of the bucket, 'I'll have to find out about that.' (28) He is anxious to understand his new surroundings, and his questions about whose house it is (12, 40 and 51), are perhaps signs of his wish to please the man who has the power to accept or reject him.

That Davies wants to stay in the house is understandable when he talks about walking to the monastery at Luton from Shepherd's Bush in poor shoes, a distance of over-thirty miles (13). All three men in the play are lonely perhaps, but Davies suffers most from loneliness, as the cruel treatment by the monk illustrates (14). Davies's story here may not be true — certainly it seems far-fetched — but it does appear likely that he feels he is spurned in this way, being treated as 'Nothing better than a dog' (15). The incident at the monastery, however, also shows him up as a scrounger, if an unfortunate one, and this, plus Mick's accusation, 'You're an old robber' (35), perhaps suggests that behind his claiming of his 'rights' (10) there is some feeling of guilt.

Davies's claim to have 'rights' is linked with his attitude towards 'aliens' (8). These may reflect his feelings of insecurity and uncertainty about where he stands in society. Such feelings imply one of the basic questions about life, that is, 'Who am I?'; but the inarticulate Davies is incapable of stating this clearly. Instead, in his search for a home, he admits to having an assumed name (20) and avoids saying where he was born (25). Mick is therefore able to alarm him by asking his name (30, 32, and 73) and saying that Davies reminds him of different people, implying that he knows his sort (31, 32 and 34).

Davies's excuses for not moving on to Sidcup (19, 51/52, 54 and 65) or to the 'caff' in Wembley (27, 39) perhaps imply a fear of the world outside the room as much as laziness. His alarm at the thought of having to answer the door as caretaker suggests this (43/44), and his reluctance to find any shoes comfortable or satisfactory, enables him to find excuses for not leaving (14, 15 and 64/65). Another factor in Davies's reluctance to move on is his age, and his self-pitying remarks often refer to his being old (9, 10, 14, 25 and 66). Mick's attack also emphasizes his age (35). There is also perhaps a hint of Aston's final attitude towards him when he says he will be getting rid of the useless sink (18). Aston is keeping several old and apparently useless things 'for the time being' (16), and Davies may be numbered among them. He may be seen as being useless, rather like his shoes, about which he says, 'they're gone, they're no good, all the good's gone out of them.' (15)

The play has, therefore, been seen by some as being partly about the rejection of the old by the young. Aston's references to his mother support this view in putting the blame for his present troubles on her. He says, 'But she signed their form' (56). Mick's aggressive claim to recognize Davies's type includes the words, 'You remind me of my uncle's brother' (31), one obvious implication of this being that Davies is like a father.

His age is also a factor in his inability to be useful in altering the house. When Mick demands expert help from him, he can only say, 'You got the wrong man.' (72) His expectations of settling into the home do not include much contribution towards its improvement, it seems. His final rejection, if it is seen as that, could therefore be considered as the discarding of the useless old man or as a sign that finding a real home implies active co-operation and unselfish friendship, qualities that Davies lacks.

'You been a good friend to me' (Davies, p.75)

Davies's comment here draws attention to what is perhaps the fundamental question underlying the play. How are people to live with each other?

We see that both Aston and Davies have good reason to be wary of other people's behaviour, Davies because he is despised and turned away, Aston because people in the café 'started being funny' (55). This helps to explain Davies's hesitation over Aston's invitation to sit down (8/9) and his assumption that he will not be allowed to stay in the room on his own (23). When left on his own, his suspicious nature leads him to search the room (28).

In act one Davies shows he is grateful for any kindness shown towards him, such as Aston's protection at the café (10). Indeed, when Aston shows concern for his comfort, he is inclined to insist that all is well, saying, for example, 'Don't you worry about that ' (19 and 21). He also says he has slept well the first night (22), and up to this point seems contented with Aston's hospitality.

24

Aston's distrust of people is evident perhaps in the hesitation he shows when offering Davies a bed (16). Nevertheless, he does appear to be seeking friendship with the old man. He gives him money (19) and keys (24), and pays for a bag of clothes for him (41). Perhaps, however, the greatest sign of friendship in this part of the play is in the growing trust Aston shows by telling Davies more and more about himself. By saying he likes the Buddha (17) and cannot drink Guinness from a thick mug (19), he reveals his unusual sensitivity. When he plans to go out he tells Davies where he is going (24) and he talks about the incident in the café which he did not understand (25). These small bits of information prepare the way for the revelation of Aston's unfortunate past, and the telling of this is probably the greatest sign of trust that Aston shows in Davies (54–57).

Aston's speech, then, can be seen as an appeal for sympathy, and Davies's reaction to it is a betrayal of the friendship that has been offered him. That Davies behaves in this way perhaps comes as no great surprise, for we have seen him abuse Aston's generosity earlier, for example, when he asks for money (26), and even in his lack of reaction to Aston's conversation about failing to get the jig-saw (39). Aston's plans to alter the house are also ignored by Davies (40/41). When Mick asks him if he is a friend of Aston's, Davies avoids agreeing (47). His selfishness, which is a contradiction of any true friendship, is seen clearly when Aston makes his complaint about sleeping badly. Davies replies, 'I slept badly' (52).

Aston's long speech seems to convince Davies in his selfish desire for security and comfort that his best hopes lie with the more powerful brother. Thus, in act three, Davies's lack of sympathy for Aston turns into open hostility. He complains to Mick about the bread knife and the gas stove (58/59). He also refers to Aston's long speech, saying, 'Since then he ain't hardly said a word.' (59) Aston, having confided in Davies and found no response, now seems to be making no more demands for his sympathy. Davies tells Mick, 'You and me, we could get this place going' (60), implying that Aston could be excluded from their plans, and now he is ready to say bluntly, 'He's no friend of mine.' (61) Now he complains that Aston prevents him from sleeping (62).

Davies's growing confidence in his superiority over Aston leads him on to his cruel attack on the older of the brothers (66/67). When he finds Aston has not listened to him, he refers to him as, 'That bastard' (66), reminding us of his words about the monk (14). His threat that Aston can be given the same medical treatment again (67) shows him to be the same as the others who have turned against Aston in the past, and by calling the shed 'stinking' (68) he throws scorn on Aston's dearest hopes.

Davies has done nothing to help Aston, apart from the unnecessary offer to 'keep an eye' on the taps (26), and although he has offered to do more for Mick (51 and 63), he has selfish motives and fails to appreciate the mutual trust and help that real friendship implies.

The title of the play implies doing a job and caring about people. Aston has been cared for in a cruel way in the hospital, and it is Davies's failure to care about Aston's troubles that separates them. Ironically, it is Davies who selfishly complains, 'He don't care about me' (59), but there is little doubt that Davies is almost wholly responsible for the situation that he finds himself in at the end. His final appeal, moreover, still shows him thinking in selfish terms as he suggests swapping beds (76) or changing the window sacking (77).

Nevertheless, the final silence of the play is a painful moment for it may suggest that the generous and friendly Aston is at last convinced of the treachery of other people and in the hopelessness of offering friendship. Against this view is the slight hope offered by the fact that we do not see Davies leave. The film version, approved by Pinter, ends with the two men still in the room, although Aston has his back turned. By this means, the decision on whether Davies should be forgiven is left with the audience.

The play, indeed, should not necessarily be interpreted as a pessimistic comment on man's inability to live unselfishly in society. What we are left with is a strong impression of the need for generosity and caring as the basis for the best sort of life.

VII Suggestions for essays

These questions are an indication of the type of question which *might* be asked in an examination; they are in no way to be regarded as 'spot' questions.

1. Make a detailed study of any *one* of the three acts showing its relation to the rest of the play.
2. Discuss the importance of Aston's long speech in relation to the rest of the play.
3. Compare and contrast the characters of the two brothers and their relationship.
4. Make a detailed study of the changes in Davies's behaviour during the play.
5. Comment on the different styles of language used by the three characters.
6. What do you think will happen after the end of the play? Support your answer with detailed references to earlier parts of the play.
7. Discuss the effect of the humour.
8. Make a detailed study of Pinter's use of silences and pauses, indicating in particular how they reveal an underlying meaning to the words being spoken.
9. Pinter has described the violence in his early plays as being not so much violence as 'a battle for positions'. Discuss.
10. Discuss the theme of menace.
11. Comment on the significance of the room.
12. Discuss the related themes of communication and failure of communication.
13. To what extent do you think that Pinter's work implies a criticism of modern society?
14. In what way would you describe Pinter's work as realistic?
15. Discuss the theme of guilt.
16. Discuss the importance of the outside world in Pinter's plays, making a detailed study of references to it.
17. Imagine you are to make a film version of the play. What changes from the stage presentation would you make. Support every change with detailed reference to the meaning of the play.

VIII Bibliography

All Pinter's plays are published by Methuen.
Poems, selected by Alan Clodd. (Enitharmon Press, 1968)

Articles and speeches by Pinter

'Writing for the Theatre' (*Evergreen Review*, No. 33, 1964), a revised version of Pinter's speech at the Seventh Annual Students' Drama Festival, Bristol, published in *The Sunday Times* (March 4, 1962) under the title 'Between the Lines'.
The Birthday Party in *Writers' Theatre*, ed. Willis Hall and Keith Waterhouse (Heinemann, 1967)
'Speech: Hamburg 1970' in *Theatre Quarterly* I, iii, 1971.

Interviews

With Kenneth Tynan (B.B.C. radio, August 19, 1960); with Harry Thompson, 'Harold Pinter Replies' (*New Theatre Magazine*, Vol. XI, 2, Jan. 1961); with Richard Findlater, 'Writing for Myself' (*Twentieth Century*, CLXIX, Feb. 1961); with Kenneth Cavander, 'Filming *The Caretaker*' (*Transatlantic Review*, No. 13, Summer 1963; reprinted in *Behind the Scenes*, comp. Joseph F. McCrindle, London, Pitman, 1971); with Marshall Pugh, 'Trying to Pin down Pinter' (*Daily Mail*, March 7, 1964); with Lawrence M. Bensky, 'The Art of the Theatre' (*The Paris Review*, No. 39, Fall 1966; reprinted in *Writers at Work*, Secker and Warburg, 1968 and Penguin 1972, and in *Theatre at Work*, ed. C. Marowitz and S. Trussler, Methuen 1967); with John Russell Taylor (*Sight and Sound*, Autumn 1966); 'Two People in a Room' (*The New Yorker*, February 25, 1967); with Henry Hewes, 'Probing Pinter's Play' (*The Saturday Review*, April 8, 1967); with Kathleen Tynan, 'In Search of Harold Pinter' (*Evening Standard*, 25 and 26 April 1968); with William Packard, (*First Stage*, VI, Summer 1968); with Michael Dean (*The Listener*, March 6, 1969); and with Joan Bakewell, 'In an Empty Bandstand' (*The Listener*, November 6, 1969).

Books on Pinter

Arnold P. Hinchliffe: *Harold Pinter* (*Twayne English Authors Series*, Twayne, New York, 1967); Walter Kerr: *Harold Pinter* (*Columbia Essays on Modern Writers*, Columbia U.P. 1967); Ronald Hayman: *Harold Pinter* (*Contemporary Playwrights Series*, Heinemann, 1968); John Russell Taylor: *Harold Pinter* (*Writers and Their Work Series*, Longmans, 1969); Lois G. Gordon: *Stratagems to Uncover Nakedness: the Dramas of Harold Pinter* (*Literary Frontiers Series*, University of Missouri Press, 1969); Martin Esslin: *The Peopled Wound, The Plays of Harold Pinter* (Methuen, 1970; reprinted in revised version as *Pinter: A Study of His Plays*, 1973); Alrene Sykes: *Harold Pinter* (Queensland U.P., 1970); James R. Hollis: *Harold Pinter: the Poetics of Silence* (S. Illinois U.P. 1970); Katherine H.

Burkman: *The Dramatic World of Harold Pinter: its Basis in Ritual* (Ohio State U.P. 1971); Arthur Ganz, ed., *Pinter, A Collection of Critical Essays (Twentieth Century Views Series*, Prentice-Hall 1972); William Baker and Stephen Ely Tabachnick: *Harold Pinter* (Oliver & Boyd 1973); Simon Trussler: *The Plays of Harold Pinter* (Gollancz 1973)

The following books have sections on Pinter

Martin Esslin: *The Theatre of the Absurd* (first published 1961; Pelican 1968); Laurence Kitchin: *Mid-Century Drama* (Faber 1962); John Russell Taylor: *Anger and After* (Penguin 1962; revised 1969); J. R. Brown and B. Harris, editors: *Stratford-upon-Avon Studies-4-Contemporary Theatre* (Arnold 1962) – this includes an essay by Clifford Leech: 'Two Romantics: Arnold Wesker and Harold Pinter'; W. A. Armstrong, ed.: *Experimental Drama* (Bell & Son 1963) – this includes an essay by M. Esslin: 'Godot and His Children: The Theatre of Samuel Beckett and Harold Pinter'; George E. Wellwarth: *The Theatre of Protest and Paradox* (New York U.P. 1964) – this includes 'Harold Pinter: the Comedy of Allusiveness'; John Kershaw: *The Present Stage* (Fontana 1966); Laurence Kitchin: *Drama in the Sixties* (Faber 1966); Frederick Lumley: *New Trends in Twentieth Century Drama* (Barrie & Rockliff 1967); Raymond Williams: *Drama from Ibsen to Brecht* (Chatto & Windus 1968); Charles Marowitz, ed.: *The Encore Reader* (Methuen 1965) includes an essay by Irvine Wardle: *'The Birthday Party'*; G. S. Fraser: *The Modern Writer and His World* (Penguin 1970); John Russell Brown: *Theatre Language* (Allen Lane, Penguin 1972); Katharine Worth: *Revolutions in Modern English Drama* (G. Bell 1972); Andrew Kennedy: *Six dramatists in search of a language* (Cambridge U.P. 1975)

Articles in journals

Modern Drama has had articles by J. Boulton (1963), F. J. Bernhard (1965), V. Amend (1967), A. Walker (1967), A. Hinchliffe (1968) and K. Burkman (1968). *The Tulane Drama Review* has had articles by Ruby Cohn (1962), Bernard F. Dukore (1962), Kelly Morris (1966), R. Schechner (1966) and John Lahr (1968). Valerie Minogue, 'Taking Care of the Caretaker' in *Twentieth Century*, 1960; Claire Sprague, 'Possible or Necessary?' in *New Theatre Magazine*, 1967.

First published in 1976 by Methuen Educational
11 New Fetter Lane, London EC4P 4EE
© 1976 College of Careers (Pty) Ltd
Printed in Great Britain by Fletcher & Son Ltd, Norwich

ISBN 0 413 34830 X

Quotations from *The Caretaker*
Copyright © 1960 by Theatre Promotions Ltd,
published by Eyre Methuen, London